BIO SOL
Gagne, Tammy. Hope Solo

T 301778

BLUE BANNER BIOGRAPHY

Hope
SOLO

Tammy Gagne

Mitchell Lane
PUBLISHERS
P.O. Box 196
Hockessin, Delaware 19707
Visit us on the web: www.mitchelllane.com
Comments? Email us: mitchelllane@mitchelllane.com

Mitchell Lane
PUBLISHERS

Printing   1   2   3   4   5   6   7   8   9

Blue Banner Biographies

Abby Wambach	Ice Cube	Miguel Tejada
Adele	Ja Rule	Mike Trout
Alicia Keys	Jamie Foxx	Nancy Pelosi
Allen Iverson	Jason Derulo	Natasha Bedingfield
Ashanti	Jay-Z	Nicki Minaj
Ashlee Simpson	Jennifer Hudson	One Direction
Ashton Kutcher	Jennifer Lopez	Orianthi
Avril Lavigne	Jessica Simpson	Orlando Bloom
Blake Lively	J. K. Rowling	P. Diddy
Blake Shelton	Joe Flacco	Peyton Manning
Bow Wow	John Legend	Pink
Brett Favre	Justin Berfield	Pit Bull
Britney Spears	Justin Timberlake	Prince William
Bruno Mars	Kanye West	Queen Latifah
CC Sabathia	Kate Hudson	Rihanna
Carrie Underwood	Katy Perry	Robert Downey Jr.
Chris Brown	Keith Urban	Robert Pattinson
Chris Daughtry	Kelly Clarkson	Ron Howard
Christina Aguilera	Kenny Chesney	Sean Kingston
Ciara	Ke$ha	Selena
Clay Aiken	Kevin Durant	Shakira
Cole Hamels	Kristen Stewart	Shia LaBeouf
Condoleezza Rice	Lady Gaga	Shontelle Layne
Corbin Bleu	Lance Armstrong	Soulja Boy Tell 'Em
Daniel Radcliffe	Leona Lewis	Stephenie Meyer
David Ortiz	Lil Wayne	Taylor Swift
David Wright	Lionel Messi	T.I.
Derek Jeter	Lindsay Lohan	Timbaland
Drew Brees	LL Cool J	Tim McGraw
Eminem	Ludacris	Tim Tebow
Eve	Mariah Carey	Toby Keith
Fergie	Mario	Usher
Flo Rida	Mary J. Blige	Vanessa Anne Hudgens
Gwen Stefani	Mary-Kate and Ashley Olsen	Will.i.am
Hope Solo	Megan Fox	Zac Efron

Library of Congress Cataloging-in-Publication Data applied for.
Gagne, Tammy.
  Hope Solo / by Tammy Gagne.
     pages cm. — (Blue banner biographies)
  Includes bibliographical references and index.
  ISBN 978-1-61228-642-6 (library bound)
  1. Solo, Hope, 1981– —Juvenile literature. 2. Women soccer players—United States—Biography—Juvenile literature. 3. Soccer goalkeepers—United States—Biography—Juvenile literature. I. Title.
  GV942.7.S6315G34 2014
  796.334092—dc23
  [B]

                                                                                  2014006902

eBook ISBN: 9781612286662

ABOUT THE AUTHOR: Tammy Gagne is the author of numerous books for adults and children, including *Day by Day with Missy Franklin* and *Mike Trout* for Mitchell Lane Publishers. She resides in northern New England with her husband and son. One of her favorite pastimes is visiting schools to speak to kids about the writing process.

PBP

Blue Banner Biography

Hope Solo celebrates the US women's soccer team's gold-medal win at the London 2012 Olympics by waving the American flag. The US team defeated Japan 2-1 to earn the gold.

Making Headlines

Drama seems to follow Hope Solo everywhere. Some of the stories are about her impressive performances on the soccer field. Others center on her very blunt remarks about her career. Further stories focus on her extraordinary personal life. No matter what the journalists (or gossip columnists) write about this well-known athlete, however, the pieces always seem to be filled with controversy.

Many people know Hope Solo as an Olympic athlete. Others may recognize her from the reality television show *Dancing with the Stars*. Still others might know that she is the wife of Jerramy Stevens, a former tight end for the Seattle Seahawks and Tampa Bay Buccaneers football teams.

Most Americans learned Hope's name when she and the rest of the US women's soccer team won the Olympic gold medal in 2008. Even before that time, though, Hope was making news in women's soccer. Often it was for her victories—like being named an All-American by *Parade* magazine in high school. But she was even making headlines for games in which she *didn't* play—like the 2007 World Cup semi-finals. Her statement about her coach's choice to bench her during that semi-finals match overshadowed the words of those who did play in that now infamous game.

Hope and her *Dancing with the Stars* partner Maksim Chmerkovskiy made it through nine weeks on the show in 2011. They were among the last four couples in the competition. Upon being voted off the show, Hope told *Extra's* Tony Dovolani that she had a wonderful time and was grateful for the experience. But she also hinted that she hadn't been treated properly. "I just don't feel like the world got to see the real me—but that's okay because I'm going back to my world where I can be myself and be respected."

Later, in her autobiography *Solo: A Memoir of Hope*, she claimed that Chmerkovskiy had mistreated her during practices. "He manhandled me in rehearsals from the start, pushing me, whacking my stomach, bending my arms

Hope Solo walks with her Dancing with the Stars *partner Maksim Chmerkovskiy outside the rehearsal studio. The pair made it into the semi-finals of the reality television competition, but were voted off on November 15, 2011.*

roughly. . . . He wanted my head in a specific position. To achieve that, he slapped me across the face. Hard." Hope claimed that ABC offered to provide her with a new dancing partner after the incident. But she says she declined, not wanting to ruin Chmerkovskiy's career. He denies Hope's claims that he treated her improperly.

In 2013, Hope and her husband Jerramy attended the 28th Anniversary Sports Spectacular Gala in Los Angeles, California. Hope received the Female Athlete of the Year Award at the event, which raised money for Cedars-Sinai Medical Center.

Hope would be part of another big story in 2012, the night before she married Jerramy Stevens. The ex-football player was no stranger to legal problems. When he was arrested for suspected assault the night before their wedding, the story made the news immediately. Without enough evidence against him, he was released and the couple was married. But negative stories about Hope and the people surrounding her were getting more attention than her accomplishments as a professional athlete.

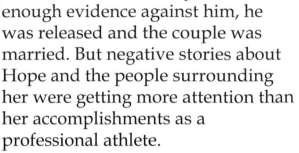

Hope shared, "With each year that's gone by and as I grow up and get older, I've become more mature, of course, but you have a sense of who you are, and you find confidence in that. . . ."

In 2013, Hope told *The Seattle Times*, "It's been a crazy year, as always—the story of my life—but it's been a great year. Right now, I'm the happiest I've ever been in my personal life. I'm happily married. Yeah, there's lots of ups and downs, but that's what makes us strong is getting through them all."

Hope never seems to worry about what people think. In an interview for the PBS documentary *Makers: Women Who Make America*, Hope shared, "With each year that's gone by and as I grow up and get older, I've become more mature, of course, but you have a sense of who you are, and you find confidence in that. . . . There are so many different walks of life, so many different personalities in the world. And no longer do you have to be a **chameleon** and try and adapt to that environment—you can truly be yourself. And if people don't like who you are, well then, it's their loss."

Hope Lost

*H*ope Amelia Solo was born on July 30, 1981, in Richland, Washington. Her mother Judy named her after a high school classmate. This older, popular girl had been especially kind to Judy, so giving the name to her infant daughter was like giving her a loving gift—hope indeed.

In many ways Hope's childhood was a lot like those of other American children. As a kid, she played in her sandbox and climbed on the jungle gym in her backyard. She had an English sheepdog, kittens, and even rabbits and turtles as pets. And she followed her older brother everywhere he went. But there was also a darker side to her early years.

Hope's father Gerry had been in prison before she was born. He had been sent there after being convicted of embezzlement. Judy had married Gerry while he was serving that sentence. He was released shortly before Hope was born. Judy had hoped that his crimes were behind him at this point.

Hope's older brother Marcus was just a toddler when his little sister came into the world. Hope also had two half-siblings from her father's first marriage. Her half-brother David and half-sister Terry lived in Kirkland, Washington, about three hours away. From the day Hope was born, they visited each summer. They even called Hope's maternal grandparents Grandma and Grandpa. Their family definitely wasn't typical. But it was a family nonetheless.

When she was little, Hope didn't think her life was that unusual. But soon she began noticing things that weren't quite right.

Terry adored Hope, treating her like a little doll in her earliest years. But it was Marcus whom Hope idolized. She wrote in *Hope Solo: My Story* (the young readers' edition of her autobiography), "If he ran, I ran. If he played baseball, I played baseball. If he rode his skateboard, I wanted to ride his skateboard—not mine, *his*, because mine was hot pink and girly and his was so much cooler. Even as a little girl, I was tough and strong."

Many of her happy memories from those early years involve physical activity. She would run alongside her mother when she would go on bike rides. Hope and her father would play basketball against her two brothers. She began playing soccer in kindergarten on a team that her father coached. "I had no problem scoring goals, even as a five-year-old," she wrote in her autobiography.

When she was little, Hope didn't think her life was that unusual. But soon she began noticing things that weren't quite right. "One spring, when I was a brownie," she wrote in *Solo: A Memoir of Hope*, "the Girl Scout Cookie money went missing. Sometimes my father went missing. One morning, my mother went out to get her car and it was gone: repossessed for lack of payment." She also remembers a big fight that erupted over her father stealing her grandfather's checkbook and writing checks to himself. Clearly Gerry's troubles were not behind them.

Gerry had trouble keeping a job. Hope and her brother relied on their mother to support the family. By the time Hope was seven years old, her parents had divorced. Soon her father would disappear for a long time. But his involvement in his kids' lives wasn't over just yet.

One day Gerry showed up, asking to take Hope and Marcus to a baseball game. But they never made it to the event. Instead, he kidnapped them. Hope told *Newsweek* magazine that they just kept driving. "We got a hotel room with a pool. We felt like we were living the life. Then I remember waking up one morning, and my dad is like, 'Baby Hope, your mom just called, and she said you can stay another three days.' And I remember being like, 'I didn't hear the phone ring.' Right then, I knew that something wasn't right."

The police caught Gerry a day or two later in a Seattle bank. A SWAT team surrounded him before taking him back to jail. Hope and her brother didn't know what to do. Scared and alone, they stayed on the city streets until Judy made it to the scene. Even though Hope knew that her father had done something wrong, she was very angry with her mother for calling the police. "I remember not talking to her the whole ride home," she told *Newsweek*. "My dad was sitting in jail. I was a confused little girl." She wouldn't see her father again for many years.

Hope makes a save during a game in Dresden, Germany, in 2011. The quarter-finals match was part of the Women's Soccer World Cup. The United States won the game against Brazil with a final score of 5 to 3, earning a spot in the semi-finals against France.

A Dual Life

Judy remarried in 1989. But neither Hope nor Marcus liked their new stepfather, Glenn. Hope wrote in her autobiography, "He barked orders at Marcus and me, made up rules, occasionally even tried to spank us." Looking back on the situation, Hope now sees that they were directing their unhappiness over the situation with their father towards Glenn. "I know now he was trying to do the right thing, but Marcus and I weren't interested in a new father, or new rules."

As Hope got older, she took comfort in playing sports. She discovered that she was very good at soccer in particular. Her natural talent combined with her hunger for winning made her one of the best forwards on the field.

Hope's grandparents, Pete and Alice Shaw, provided some much-needed stability in their grandchildren's lives at this time. They attended all of Hope's sporting events and other school activities. They even brought her to soccer tournaments in their camper so they had a place to pass time between games.

As Hope moved into middle school, her relationship with her mother got worse. The two fought often. Around this time, Marcus had begun starting fights and getting into trouble at school. By the time he had entered high school, he'd earned himself a reputation as a troublemaker. Their mother had to give extra time and attention to Marcus and the trouble he caused, and Hope felt neglected.

When Hope had to write a paper for school about what she wanted to be when she grew up, another dream was born. "I am going to be a professional soccer player."

She dealt with the things in her life that weren't going well by imagining an alternate reality. As unlikely as they were, these fantasies helped get Hope's mind off her unpleasant family situation. Many nights she would lie in bed and picture running away and finding her father so that they could live together once again.

When Hope had to write a paper for school about what she wanted to be when she grew up, another dream was born. "I am going to be a professional soccer player," she wrote decisively. It seemed as likely as her dream of creating a new life with her estranged father. "I was dreaming for something that didn't even exist," Hope recalled in her autobiography. "This was years before the 1996 Summer Olympics, when the US women's soccer team first entered the nation's consciousness. This was long before any kind of professional women's league had been established." But it was a hint of what was to come for the young girl who liked to play what was considered a boy's sport.

Hope also played basketball in middle school. She had excellent hand-eye coordination and leaping skills. Although she had sharpened these abilities on the basketball court, they would soon prove helpful to her in soccer as well. While most soccer players cannot use their hands, goalies can. And there was a shortage of players for this important position in the Olympic Development Program (ODP) that Hope wanted to join when she was thirteen.

When the coaches asked her to try playing goalie, Hope was open to the idea. "I was game," she wrote in her autobiography. "I just wanted to make the team. I batted away shots, dove to make saves, and easily made my team. But then an older team—three levels up—decided they wanted me for a backup goalkeeper and cherry-picked me off my age-group team."

Thirteen-year-old Hope was pleased to be playing alongside sixteen-year-olds. But her family was not nearly as happy. In youth soccer the goalkeeping position is often filled with the least athletic kids. Hope's mother and grandmother saw the position as an insult. They thought that she should be playing forward instead. They also worried about her safety. One of the most common injuries for goalies was a concussion from colliding with one of the other team's forwards.

But Hope continued to play goalkeeper for her ODP team. Back at school, however, she was a forward. Being able to play both positions helped her become a much better athlete. In many ways it was the best of both worlds for a young athlete with Olympic dreams. "I learned both ends of the field," she wrote in her autobiography. "Knowing how a forward attacks is an advantage for a goalkeeper. It was as if I had a double identity—my Richland life and my expanding outside world as a successful goalkeeper."

Hope Solo kicks the ball during a quarter-finals game of the 2012 Olympic Games in London between the United States and New Zealand.

CHAPTER 4

Saving Games— and Relationships

Hope often traveled all over Washington for soccer games. One Sunday she rode with a friend to a game in Seattle when she saw someone familiar in the parking lot. After all the years of dreaming about finding her father, he was now within shouting distance. "He was walking away, so I approached him," she told *Newsweek*. At first Hope worried that he wouldn't recognize her because it had been so long. But he instantly opened his arms and hugged her.

He watched her game, then asked her if she wanted to see where he lived. Gerry led his daughter and the friend she had ridden to the game with to a makeshift tent in the woods. He was homeless. "I hadn't had much experience with homeless people," Hope wrote in her book, "yet I wasn't completely shocked."

Hope asked her father if he would come to some of her games. She wanted him to see what a capable athlete she was becoming. He promised that he would.

As Hope moved on to high school, she continued playing both basketball and soccer. She scored a total of 109 goals for Richland High School as a forward in the latter sport. She was also named an All-American by *Parade* magazine, twice.

Soon she started catching the eyes of college recruiters. Schools from all over the country were sending her letters. Some schools tried to lure her with promises of being able to play basketball as well as soccer. Others told her that she could play both goalkeeper and forward. But the common thread was the goalie position. All of the schools wanted Hope in their nets.

Some schools tried to lure her with promises of being able to play basketball as well as soccer. Others told her that she could play both goalkeeper and forward.

Hope always figured that she would choose a faraway college. Many people tried to get her to do just that. It wasn't until she made a visit to the University of Washington that she decided to stay closer to home. "I suddenly realized that this was my corner of the country, where I belonged," she wrote in *Solo: A Memoir of Hope*. "I felt a rush of emotion and a click of recognition so strong that it forced me to sit down hard on the stairs. I wanted to be more than a one-dimensional athlete, a number on a jersey, a prize to be attained by some coach."

When Hope graduated from high school in 1999, her father was in the audience. Her half-sister Terry had brought him with her to witness his younger daughter's milestone. She was a little nervous about the idea of going to college so close to where he now lived. She wondered if he would become a bigger part of her life. She also worried about what her new classmates would think if they knew that her father was a homeless person.

In 1999, Hope graduated from high school and decided to stay in Washington for college. She would now play for the University of Washington Huskies soccer team.

When it came time to move to the UW campus, Hope's mother made the trip with her. Before the day was over, they both teared up. In the young readers' edition of her autobiography, Hope wrote, "I had never said goodbye to my mother in my whole life. It was my father who was always disappearing. Mom was the one who had always been there. She was the one who had been left with two kids, the one who had to support us and deal with all the problems. . . . She wasn't perfect, but she had tried her hardest. Despite all the harsh words and fights between us, she was the one I knew would never walk out on me."

In all she led her team to 18 shutouts and made 325 saves during her college career. And to this day, she still holds the university's records for both.

While Hope attended UW, her father made good on his promise. At times he walked miles to see his daughter's games. He attended every one of them. Around this time she would bring food to his tent in the woods, happy to have a relationship with her father once again. "I was finding I really enjoyed his company," she wrote in the young readers' edition of her book. "I knew that I hated being judged by others, so I did my best not to judge him but simply appreciate him for who he was."

Hope had begun playing for UW unsure of whether she wanted to give up being a field player. She intentionally chose the number 18 for her team jersey to keep her options open. (Most goalies wear the number 1.) She enjoyed scoring goals and winning games. Those were hard things to give up. But one day her goalkeeper coach gave her a note that changed her perspective. It read, "A goalkeeper cannot win a game. She can only save it." And that she did, many times over.

As a goalie for the Washington Huskies, Hope raked in the honors. She earned the NSCAA All-American award her sophomore, junior, and senior year. She was also named the Pac-10 Women's Soccer Player of the Year as a junior. In all she led her team to 18 shutouts and made 325 saves during her college career. And to this day, she still holds the university's records for both.

The decision to become a full-time goalie was a difficult one. Hope enjoyed scoring goals. But she also had an undeniable talent for making saves. Ultimately, she decided that the net was where she wanted to be. She is seen here making one of her famous saves in a game against Japan at the 2012 Olympics in London, England. The US won the game with a final score of 2 to 1.

As a member of the Philadelphia Charge, Hope defends against Cindy Parlow in a game with the Atlanta Beat in Villanova, Pennsylvania, in 2003.

Striking Gold

*B*y Hope's senior year, she had become one of the top players in the country. She was invited to attend the 2003 WUSA (Women's United Soccer Association) draft in Atlanta, Georgia. Hope was chosen as the fourth pick. The little girl who had said she would become a professional soccer player when she grew up was going to make that dream a reality by playing for the Philadelphia Charge in the professional league's third season.

Hope also wanted to be part of the 2004 US Olympic Team in Athens. But as an alternate, she never made it into a game there. The 2008 Olympics would be a different story. But before that chance would present itself, Hope would find herself on the bench once again.

During the 2007 World Cup semi-finals, Hope's coach decided to put Briana Scurry in the net instead of her. Hope was angry. And she didn't hide it. "The game was a disaster almost from the start," Hope later wrote in *Solo: A Memoir of Hope*. The US team lost 4 to 0.

Following the game, Hope criticized her coach's call. She told *Newsweek*, "It was the wrong decision, and I think

Hope sits (far right) with her United States teammates (from left to right) Lindsay Tarpley, Marian Dalmy, Angela Hucles, Nicole Barnhart, and Marci Jobson at the FIFA 2007 World Cup semi-finals match. The US lost the game to Brazil with a final score of 4 to 0. The loss sent Brazil into the finals with Germany.

anybody who knows anything about the game knows that. There's no doubt in my mind I would have made those saves." Her statement angered many people including her coach, fellow players, and even some of her fans. To them it seemed that she had betrayed her teammate by blaming her for the loss.

But Hope feels she had a right to speak her mind that day. "One thing I've learned in my life is that I can speak for myself . . . " she wrote in her autobiography. "If I had meekly accepted what others told me, my life would be radically different: I would have gone to a different school. I never would have reconnected with my father. I would be estranged from my mother. I would have viewed myself as a failure."

In a 2013 interview with the website Goal.com, Hope made it clear that she isn't on the soccer field to make friends. "I think people have different definitions of team unity. My definition is doing whatever it takes to win, what makes a great team, it's performance on the field, respect on the field. Unity doesn't mean that we as women go to the movies and go shopping together."

The year 2007 hadn't been a good one for Hope. In June her father had died suddenly of a heart attack. Hope was heartbroken. But she was determined to keep working toward her goals.

When the 2008 Olympic trials came around, Hope earned herself a full-fledged spot on the US Team. And she wasn't about to waste the chance before her. She helped her team—and her country—bring home the gold medal from Beijing, China. In the moments after Team USA's win, Hope's first phone call was to Marcus. He and his fiancée had just become parents and therefore could not make the trip to see Hope play in person. "We did it! We did it!" she shouted into the phone. No one was happier for her than her big brother—her biggest fan.

She followed up the 2008 victory with a repeat performance at the 2012 Summer Olympic Games in London, England. Hope and her American teammates won the gold medal yet again in the final game against the women's team from Japan with a score of 2 to 1.

Hope and her teammates were thrilled. When asked about Hope's performance in the net, Carli Lloyd told the *Tampa Bay Times*, "She's the best goalkeeper ever on the planet. That's what she does. She comes up big in big moments. She's just unbelievable. She's the best ever."

Teammate Megan Rapinoe agreed. "Every time they took a shot, she was there," she told the *Tampa Bay Times*.

Hope offers some tips to 11-year-old Hannah Prouty of Issaquah, Washington. The two met at the University of Washington Soccer Camp in Seattle. Like Hope, Hannah plays the goalkeeper position. Hope attended the event as part of the Gatorade Beat the Heat program, which teaches kids about the importance of heat safety and proper hydration in sports.

"She's the best goaltender in the world. I don't even think that's a discussion anymore. Yeah, she does a lot of talking, but that's who she is. We've accepted that."

And in her trademark style, Hope spoke her mind following the win. "I don't care how people perceive me," she told the *Tampa Bay Times*. "I am who I am. I'm here to win. It's not always pretty, and I don't know when I'm going to be asked to step up, the first game or last game. At some point it's going to come down to the goaltender. I think I tend to play well under pressure, but a lot of great players do."

Since Hope was first drafted in 2003, professional women's soccer leagues have come and gone in the United States. She played professionally overseas in Sweden and France, and back at home in Saint Louis, Atlanta, and Boca Raton, Florida. Hope began playing for the Seattle Reign in 2013. The team is part of the new National Women's Soccer League.

In 2012 Hope joined forces with the Game Changers program. The charity partnered professional athletes with their local communities to fulfill the needs of people in the community. In Hope's case, that meant visiting patients at the Seattle Children's Hospital. She told ESPN, "I grew up here, went to college here and am back playing professionally here, so nothing would make me happier than to give back to Seattle."

Amidst all her awards and victories, Hope has earned the right to her self-confidence. But in many ways she is also **humble**. "Every morning," she wrote in *Hope Solo: My Story*, "I wake up feeling blessed. I'm filled with graciousness to be able to travel the world, live life to the fullest, and play the game I love."

1981	Hope Solo is born in Richland, Washington.
1988	Hope's parents divorce.
1989	Hope's mother Judy remarries.
1995–1999	Hope plays forward on her high school soccer team; *Parade* magazine names her an All-American, twice.
1999	Hope graduates from Richland High School; she enrolls at the University of Washington and begins playing goalkeeper for the Washington Huskies.
2000–2003	Hope wins NSCAA All-American honors, three times.
2003	Hope sets school records for shutouts and saves; She is chosen by the Philadelphia Charge in the WUSA draft.
2004	Hope is chosen as an alternate for the Summer Olympics in Athens, Greece.
2007	Hope is benched for the World Cup semi-finals; she publicly calls her coach's decision a mistake.
2008	Hope and her US teammates win the gold medal in women's soccer at the Summer Olympics in Beijing, China.
2011	Hope wins the Golden Glove award at the World Cup as the United States places second; she appears on *Dancing with the Stars* and earns fourth place in the competition.
2012	Hope helps Team USA bring home another gold medal in soccer at the Summer Olympics in London, England; she publishes her autobiographies, *Solo: A Memoir of Hope* and *Hope Solo: My Story*. Hope marries ex-football player Jerramy Stevens.
2014	Hope Solo called to training camp by US Women's National team coach, Tom Sermanni.

AWARDS

1997–1998	*Parade* All-American (twice)
1999	Record for high school career goals (109) in Big Nine Conference; Washington state championship winner
2000–2003	NSCAA All-American (three times)
2001	Nominated for the Hermann Trophy; Pac-10 Women's Soccer Player of the Year
2002	Nordic Cup winner with US Under-21 team
2003	University of Washington's all-time leader in shutouts (18), saves (325), goals against average (1.02), and career shutouts (18)
2006	Best Goalkeeper in Algarve Cup
2008	Olympic Gold Medalist (Beijing)
2009	US Soccer Female Athlete of the Year; first goalkeeper to be named MVP of Algarve Cup; WPS (Women's Professional Soccer) Goalkeeper of the Year; WPS All-Star
2010	Most saves in the WPS; WPS All-Star
2011	Women's World Cup Runner-Up; World Cup Golden Glove and Bronze Ball Winner
2012	Olympic Gold Medalist (London)
2013	Sports Spectacular Female Athlete of the Year

FURTHER READING

Find Out More

Bankston, John. *Abby Wambach*. Hockessin, DE: Mitchell Lane Publishers, 2014.

Lisi, Clemente A. *The U.S. Women's Soccer Team: An American Success Story*. Lanham, MD: Scarecrow Press, 2013.

Solo, Hope. *Hope Solo: My Story* (Young Readers' Edition). New York: HarperCollins, 2012.

On the Internet

Biography.com: Hope Solo
http://www.biography.com/people/hope-solo-20883135

Makers: Hope Solo
http://www.makers.com/hope-solo

US Soccer: Hope Solo
http://www.ussoccer.com/teams/wnt/s/hope-solo.aspx

Works Consulted

Dovolani, Tony. Interview with Hope Solo. *Extra*, November 15, 2011.

Gillin, Joshua. "Solo Blasts 'DWTS' Partner." *Tampa Bay Times*, August 18, 2012.

Hoppes, Lynne. "Shaun Phillips, Hope Solo Work Together on Charity." *ESPN Page 2*, April 2, 2012. http://espn.go.com/espn/page2/index?id=7766480

Labidou, Alex. "Hope Solo: Sermanni a Better Communicator than Sundhage." Goal.com, August 13, 2013. http://www.goal.com/en-us/news/1698/womens-soccer/2013/08/13/4184453/hope-solo-sermanni-a-better-communicator-than-sundhage

Mayers, Joshua. "Hope Solo: 'I'm the Happiest I've Ever Been in My Personal Life. I'm Happily Married.'" *Seattle Times*, January 24, 2013. http://seattletimes.com/html/sounders/2020208436_reign25.html

McGee, Dyllan, Betsy West, and Peter Kunhardt. *Makers: Women Who Make America*. Kunhardt McGee Productions, 2013. DVD.

Romano, Andrew. "U.S. Olympic Soccer Goalie Hope Solo Speaks." *Newsweek*, July 16, 2012. http://www.newsweek.com/us-olympic-soccer-goalie-hope-solo-speaks-65527

Shelton, Gary. "Gary Shelton at the Games: Goalie Hope Solo Shows Why She Was U.S.'s Best Hope in Gold-Medal Win over Japan." *Tampa Bay Times*, August 9, 2012. http://www.tampabay.com/sports/olympics/gary-shelton-at-the-games-goalie-hope-solo-shows-why-she-was-uss-best-hope/1245113

Solo, Hope. *Hope Solo: My Story* (Young Readers' Edition). New York: HarperCollins, 2012.

Solo, Hope. *Solo: A Memoir of Hope*. New York: HarperCollins, 2012.

INDEX